To the Teacher

This handwriting book is not for elementary school st ... ...for those who have reached adolescence, or even adulthood, without mastering cursive handwriting. Often such students avoid written work altogether and fail to turn in assignments that require writing. Sometimes they are misdiagnosed as dysgraphic and typing is prescribed. However, there are good reasons for persisting with handwriting. In the first place, in many situations the typewriter or the computer is simply not available. Second, the writing process, the "motor memory," is still the best way of reinforcing learning and is an integral part of any multi-sensory approach to learning to read and to spell. Finally, with an older student, improvement is nearly always rapid and the results more than justify the time and energy expended.

This workbook is divided into three stages: pre-writing exercises, lowercase formations, and uppercase formations. Pages for practice in joining certain combinations and in copying are also included.

The pre-writing exercises provide training in correct posture, pencil grip, and paper position. For students who have formed inefficient habits, the process may involve training a different set of muscles. These initial exercises should therefore be done under the supervision of the teacher or tutor. Once students have established the correct grip, paper position, and posture, they can practice on their own.

Students should be encouraged to do all the letter formation exercises slowly and carefully. Those who have been in the habit of scribbling will have to make a conscious effort to slow down. For this reason, the amount of practice needs to be limited; a student cannot, especially at first, be expected to complete a whole row of a single letter carefully. Start with three to five copies of each letter. Some students will need more drill than can be provided in this workbook. All the exercises can be repeated on separate sheets of paper, especially the pre-writing exercises with which each writing session should begin.

Lowercase letters should be mastered before uppercase letters are started. Students of high school age should be able to write the alphabet neatly in about twenty seconds. Capitals are much more difficult because they begin in many different places and directions. The models offered here are simplified versions, likely to maintain their legibility. Permit variations only when there is a good reason for doing so.

Once mastery has been achieved, students need to continue to practice, writing at least one lowercase and one uppercase alphabet daily. This workbook provides some copying exercises. Students who need to practice copying printed words into cursive or joining certain letter combinations correctly should use any book that provides lists of words.* For others, copying short selections of poetry or perhaps making a personal book of favorite quotations will be appropriate.

*C. Wilson Anderson, Jr., *A Workbook of Resource Words for Phonetic Reading*, Books 1 and 2 (Cambridge, Mass.: Educators Publishing Service, Inc., 1980).

To the Student

Before you begin to improve your handwriting skills, check three important details: the position of your paper, your posture, and your pencil grip.

Paper position is crucial. The paper must be slanted at a forty-five-degree angle—no more and no less. As your hand swings across the paper, your elbow acts as a pivot. If the paper is slanted too much, the words will fall below the line; if it is not slanted enough, they will fly off the line. Strips of tape attached to your desk like train tracks can help maintain the correct position. Another trick, invented by a student of mine, is to turn under the bottom corner of the paper and to keep the resulting edge parallel to the edge of the table.

Your posture is also important. Be sure to sit up straight with both elbows on the desk and both feet on the floor. As you write, your left hand should rest at the top of the paper and move it upward. It acts like the roller on a typewriter, allowing your right hand to remain in the same position on the desk. Both elbows should be on the desk all the time.

Last, check your pencil grip. Your pencil should be held between your index finger and thumb and should rest on your middle finger. The eraser should be pointing to your right shoulder.

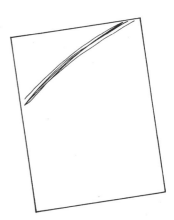

Not sufficiently slanted

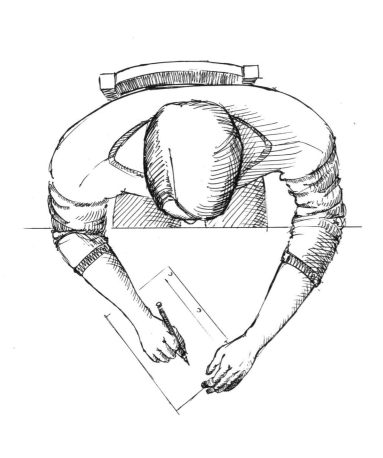

Correct paper position

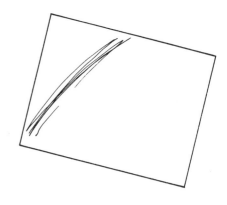

Slanted too far

Correct writing position

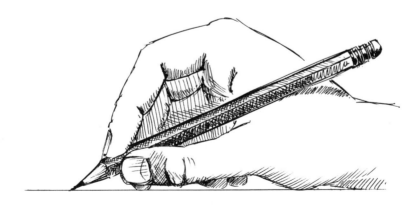

Correct pencil grip

Position your paper carefully. Pivot on your elbow so that your forearm acts like a windshield wiper. Relax. Trace and copy all the way down the paper.

Now try to make wind tunnels. Be sure your pencil points toward your shoulder. Fill the page.

Alternate between windshield wipers and wind tunnels.

Push up and pull down with your arm as you do this push-pull exercise.

MMMMMMMMMMMMMMMMMMMMMMMMMMMMMMMMMMMW

Alternate between windshield wipers and push-pull.

This is harder. Take your time and use your whole arm, not just your fingers.

Same, but upside down.

Alternate.

Put the two together.

Try this.

Marion Richardson, *Writing and Writing Patterns* (Sevenoaks, Kent, England: Hodder & Stoughton Educational, n.d.). Reprinted by permission of the publisher.

Here are two more to try.

Marion Richardson, *Writing and Writing Patterns* (Sevenoaks, Kent, England: Hodder & Stoughton Educational, n.d.). Reprinted by permission of the publisher.

When you practiced *ᴜᴜᴜᴜᴜᴜᴜᴜᴜ* , you were practicing the·upstrokes for the letters below. Trace first. Then practice upstrokes and letters three times each.

b	p
e	r
f	s
h	t
i	u
j	v
k	w
l	y

b   e   f   h   i   j   k   l

p   r   s   t   u   v   w   y

When you practiced *mmmmmm* , you were practicing the up-strokes for the rest of the letters.

a

c

d

g

m

n

o

q

x

z

a c d g m n o q x z

Remember, all lowercase letters begin on the line.

Practice the whole alphabet. Begin and end your letters carefully.

a .	.	.	*n* .	.	.
b .	.	.	*o* .	.	.
c .	.	.	*p* .	.	.
d .	.	.	*q* .	.	.
e .	.	.	*r* .	.	.
f .	.	.	*s* .	.	.
g .	.	.	*t* .	.	.
h .	.	.	*u* .	.	.
i .	.	.	*v* .	.	.
j .	.	.	*w* .	.	.
k .	.	.	*x* .	.	.
l .	.	.	*y* .	.	.
m .	.	.	*z* .	.	.

There are four bridge letters: *b, o, v,* and *w.* They need special care. Be sure to make the bridges saucer shaped. Practice just the bridges.

Now practice the letters.

Look at what you've done. Circle the best of each letter. Try again.

Try the whole alphabet again. Make the bridge letters carefully.

a.   .   .   .   *n.*   .   .   .

b.   .   .   .   *o.*   .   .   .

c.   .   .   .   *p.*   .   .   .

d.   .   .   .   *q.*   .   .   .

e.   .   .   .   *r.*   .   .   .

f.   .   .   .   *s.*   .   .   .

g.   .   .   .   *t.*   .   .   .

h.   .   .   .   *u.*   .   .   .

i.   .   .   .   *v.*   .   .   .

j.   .   .   .   *w.*   .   .   .

k.   .   .   .   *x.*   .   .   .

l.   .   .   .   *y.*   .   .   .

m.   .   .   .   *z.*   .   .   .

This is a tricky group of letters. The lines cross above the line: ℓ not $\mathcal{L}$. Go forward ╱ and straight down ℓ.

ℓ

ℓ

h

f

k is a specially difficult letter. Practice it large first.

k

k

k

ℓ

h

f

k

a and *o* are a troublesome pair. Both letters are *oval,* not round. *o* stops at midnight. Practice leaving a gap.

o

o

o

a stops at two o'clock. Practice leaving a gap.

a

a

a

Now close the gaps.

a

o

a

o

Next practice carefully. Watch out for difficult letters (starred).

*a.   .   .   .   n.   .   .   .

*b.   .   .   .   *o.   .   .   .

c.   .   .   .   p.   .   .   .

d.   .   .   .   q.   .   .   .

e.   .   .   .   r.   .   .   .

*f.   .   .   .   s.   .   .   .

g.   .   .   .   t.   .   .   .

*h.   .   .   .   u.   .   .   .

i.   .   .   .   v.   .   .   .

j.   .   .   .   w.   .   .   .

*k.   .   .   .   x.   .   .   .

l.   .   .   .   y.   .   .   .

m.   .   .   .   z.   .   .   .

The numerals *4* and *5* are formed with two strokes.

∟ 4   5 5

8 is best made starting like *S* and then finishing it: S 8

None of the numbers start on the line—they all begin at the top.

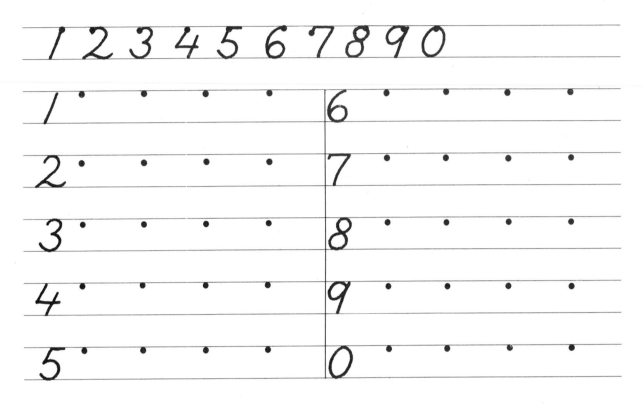

1 2 3 4 5 6 7 8 9 0

1.

2.

3.

Four letters finish later. Write the word; then go back.

i			
in			
it			
him			
slip			
j			
job			
jam			
joke			
jelly			
t			
ton			
that			
battle			
stop			
x			
exit			
exam			
extent			
xylem			

Bridge letters are difficult to join. Practice these connections with *o*.

oa	*on*
ob	*oo*
oc	*op*
od	*oq*
oe	*or*
of	*os*
og	*ot*
oh	*ou*
oi	*ov*
oj	*ow*
ok	*ox*
ol	*oy*
om	*oz*

Be sure to make *a* and *o* carefully on this page.

talk			
shape			
mold			
comb			
float			
coach			
boat			
come			
came			
word			
ward			
bond			
band			

More practice with bridges.

o out			
cope			
home			
most			
over			
b but			
bake			
brain			
best			
table			
v very			
vine			
over			
vote			
love			
w we			
who			
away			
down			
wind			

Final practice—write five times.

a b c d e f g h i j k l m

n o p q r s t u v w x y z

1.

2.

3.

4.

5.

Capitals are difficult because they start in so many different places. Practice the groups below.

This is the largest group. Begin with a walking stick.

$\mathcal{7 M \ 7 \quad 7 \quad 7}$

$\mathcal{7 N \ 7 \quad 7 \quad 7}$

$\mathcal{7 U \ 7 \quad 7 \quad 7}$

$\mathcal{7 V \ 7 \quad 7 \quad 7}$

$\mathcal{7 Y \ 7 \quad 7 \quad 7}$

$\mathcal{7 W \ 7 \quad 7 \quad 7}$

$\mathcal{7 K \ 7 \quad 7 \quad 7}$

$\mathcal{7 H \ 7 \quad 7 \quad 7}$

Begin with a little upstroke and then move down.

$\mathcal{1 B \ 1 \quad 1 \quad 1}$

$\mathcal{1 P \ 1 \quad 1 \quad 1}$

$\mathcal{1 R \ 1 \quad 1 \quad 1}$

Begin at the top and move counterclockwise.

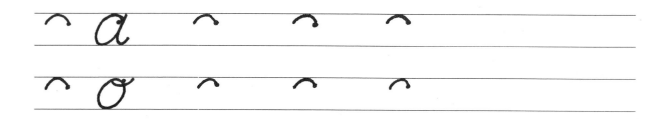

Move along the top line first and then go down.

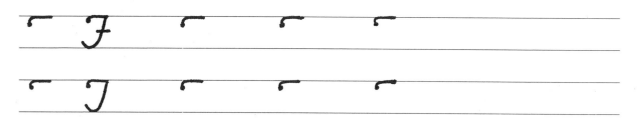

Start on the line and go forward.

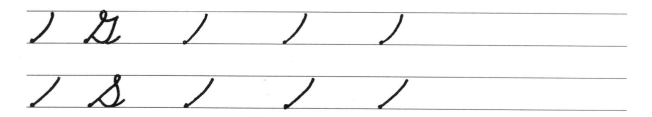

Start on the line and go backward.

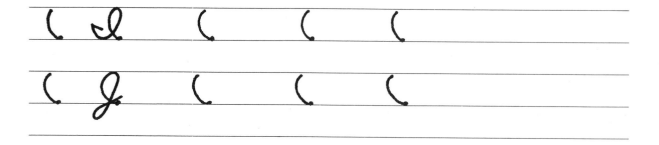

Start forward and loop over.

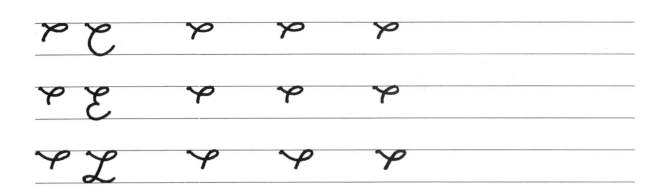

Start at the top and go straight down.

Begin like a number *2*. *Q* is always followed by *u*.

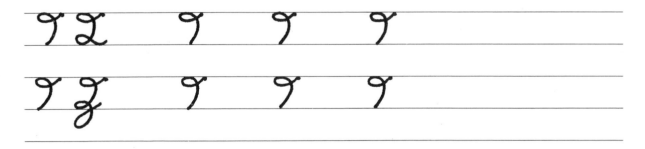

Begin like lowercase *x* but near the top.

Practice all of the capitals. Watch where they begin.

$\frown$ $\mathcal{a}$	γ $\mathcal{N}$
$\mathcal{B}$	$\frown$ $\mathcal{O}$
$\mathcal{C}$	$\mathcal{P}$
$\mathcal{D}$	$\mathcal{Q}$
$\mathcal{E}$	$\mathcal{R}$
$\mathcal{F}$	$\mathcal{S}$
$\mathcal{G}$	$\mathcal{T}$
$\mathcal{H}$	$\mathcal{U}$
$\mathcal{I}$	$\mathcal{V}$
$\mathcal{J}$	$\mathcal{W}$
$\mathcal{K}$	$\mathcal{X}$
$\mathcal{L}$	$\mathcal{Y}$
$\mathcal{M}$	$\mathcal{Z}$

Try again.

a	n
B	O
C	P
D	Q
E	R
F	S
G	T
H	U
I	V
J	W
K	X
L	Y
M	Z

Practice the whole alphabet.

A B C D E F G H I J K L M

N O P Q R S T U V W X Y Z

1.

2.

3.

4.

5.

Alternate.

a b c d e f g h i j k l m

n o p q r s t u v w x y z

A B C D E F G H I J K L M

N O P Q R S T U V W X Y Z

1. _____

_____

_____

_____

_____

_____

_____

_____

2. _____

_____

_____

_____

_____

_____

_____

_____

Most capitals join with the next letter, but *seven* do not. Practice these letters and words carefully.

D		
Do		
Dog		
Dust		
Daisy		
Diane		
David		
O		
On		
Over		
Out		
Olaf		
Olivia		

Practice these letters and words carefully.

P		
Put		
Plan		
Phone		
Paula		
T		
Tuesday		
Tina		
Trust		
Thursday		
V		
Very		
Voice		

Practice these letters and words carefully.

Victoria		
Visit		
View		
W		
West		
When		
William		
Washington		
X		
Xylem		
Xerxes		
Xenophobia		

Practice writing these words. Watch out for the seven that don't join.

And	No
Be	Over
Can	Put
Do	Quit
Ever	Rob
For	So
Go	This
Her	Up
It	Very
Just	Why
Kite	Xylem
Let	Yes
Me	Zebra

Practice everything you know.

Lowercase alphabet:

_____

_____

_____

_____

Uppercase alphabet:

_____

_____

_____

_____

Numerals from 1 to 20:

_____

_____

_____

_____

Look back at the pages before this one. Then practice anything you have forgotten.

_____

_____

_____

Now you know it all; all you need is practice. Every day do a page like this with lowercase letters, uppercase letters, and numerals. Then do one of the following pages. The more you practice, the better you'll get.

Names:

Colin

Tony

Amy

Rosa

Tracy

Lee

Eddie

Marie

Lisa

Josephine

Kelly

Sally

Mike

Days of the week and holidays:

Monday

Tuesday

Wednesday

Thursday

Friday

Saturday

Sunday

Fourth of July

Columbus Day

New Year's Eve

Labor Day

Halloween

Months of the year:

January

February

March

April

May

June

July

August

September

October

November

December

Abbreviations:

Mr.

Mrs.

Mr. and Mrs.

Ms.

M. D.

Jr.

P. O. Box

R. S. V. P.

U. S. A.

St.

Ave.

Inc.

Co.

Ways to begin and end a friendly letter:

Dear Sylvia,

Dear Peter,

Dear Mr. Wong,

Dear Dr. Jones,

Love,

Yours sincerely,

Ways to begin and end a business letter:

Dear XYZ Company:

Dear Dr. Lopez:

Yours sincerely,

Yours truly,

Titles of books are underlined. Capitalize the first word and all the important words.

Hamlet   _Romeo and Juliet_

Animal Farm   _The Great Gatsby_

Dune   _Born Free_

Of Mice and Men   _Great Expectations_

The Pigman   _Gone with the Wind_

The Outsiders   _Cannery Row_

Titles of short stories and poems are capitalized and placed in *quotation marks,* not underlined.

"The Lottery"

"The Blue Hotel"

"Paul Revere's Ride"

"The Pit and the Pendulum"

"The Gift of the Magi"

"Miniver Cheevy"

Famous dyslexics:

Thomas Edison

Woodrow Wilson

Amy Lowell

Harvey Cushing

Nelson Rockefeller

Leonardo da Vinci

H. C. Andersen

Bruce Jenner

Susan Hampshire

Winston Churchill

Auguste Rodin

Ringo Starr

Pablo Picasso

Baseball teams:

New York Yankees

Detroit Tigers

Boston Red Sox

Chicago Cubs

New York Mets

Oakland A's

Montreal Expos

Baltimore Orioles

Texas Rangers

Houston Astros

Chicago White Sox

San Diego Padres

Rock and folk groups:

The Rolling Stones

The Who

The Grateful Dead

The Beatles

The Kingston Trio

Peter, Paul and Mary

Add your three favorites.